THE BATTLE OF BRITAIN

THE BATTLE OF BRITAIN

NIGEL CAWTHORNE

ARCTURUS

This edition published in 2012 by Arcturus Publishing Limited
26/27 Bickels Yard, 151–153 Bermondsey Street,
London SE1 3HA

Copyright © 2010 Arcturus Publishing Limited

ISBN: 978-1-84837-565-9
AD001544EN

Printed in China

FRONTISPIECE image Three Supermarine Spitfire Mk.I aircraft of 19 Squadron. The Spitfire, which only entered service in 1938, proved the winning weapon of the Battle of Britain.

CONTENTS

INTRODUCTION: BEFORE THE STORM   6

COUNTDOWN   22

THE MEN AND THEIR MACHINES   50

THE ENEMY ABOVE   78

COMMAND AND CONTROL   102

THE FEW   122

THEIR FINEST HOUR   144

THE FINAL VICTORY   194

INDEX   206

PICTURE CREDITS   208

BEFORE THE STORM

BRITAIN was not ready to go to war in September 1939. Eleven months before, the British prime minister Neville Chamberlain had made a peace deal with Adolf Hitler at a conference in Munich and had flown home proclaiming "peace for our time". However, it was clear that Hitler could not be trusted when he said he had "no further territorial demands in Europe" as, in March 1939, he swallowed the rest of Czechoslovakia. Two weeks later Britain and France had guaranteed the independence of Poland. But in August, Germany and the Soviet Union signed a non-aggression pact with secret clause agreeing the division of Poland.

Then on 1 September 1939, fifty-five German divisions rolled over the Polish border and Britain and France declared war.

Little could be done to aid Poland. The French launched an offensive into Saarland, but halted it after ten days. Six months of relative inaction followed. Meanwhile, Britain prepared itself for war and sent an Expeditionary Force to France. In April 1940, Hitler invaded Denmark. Then, as the German army stormed into Belgium and the Netherlands, Chamberlain resigned and Winston Churchill became Prime Minister.

The main attack on France came on 10 May. Some 1,500,000 men with over 1,500 tanks

German troops enter the Polish tow
of Lodz and are greeted by members
the town's considerable ethnic Germa
community, September 193

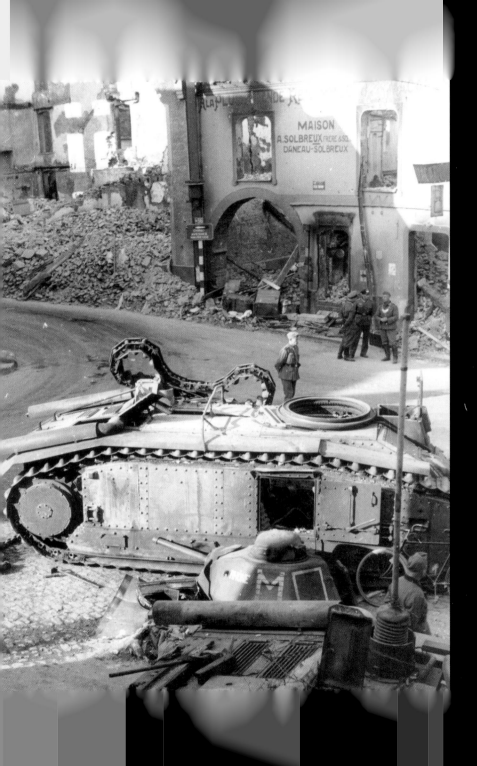

pushed through the dense and hilly forest of the Ardennes, which the French had thought unsuitable for large-scale operations. Defences there were rudimentary. The German thrust was supported by a thousand planes. The French had just a handful aloft.

The German advance split the French Army in two. It then turned west towards the Channel coast, encircling the British Army, which fell back on the port of Dunkirk. For reasons still obscure, Hitler halted the Panzers for two days. This gave the British time to consolidate their defences and evacuate some 340,000 men, many of them on small craft whose owners had volunteered for the Channel crossing. Another 220,000 Allied troops were later rescued by British ships from Cherbourg, Saint-Malo, Brest, and Saint-Nazaire in north-western France. In just three weeks, the Germans had taken more than a million

men prisoner. But the bulk of Britain's most experienced troops had been saved, seemingly by a miracle. This withdrawal was regarded as a reprieve by the British.

Although most of the British Expeditionary Force was now safely back in Britain, the Battle of France was not over. On 5 June the German Army turned south. Two days later, they broke through at Rouen. On 12 June, the French commander General Maxime Weygand told prime minister Paul Reynaud that the Battle of France was lost. On 14 June, the Germans entered Paris and drove on rapidly to the south. The French government fled to Tours then to Bordeaux, where Reynaud resigned on 16 June. He was replaced by his deputy, the elderly Marshal Philippe Pétain, France's most honoured soldier in World War I. That night, Pétain's government requested an armistice. While the two sides

LEFT British anti-aircraft guns lie abandoned on the seafront at Dunkirk, after the evacuation and defenders lay dead.

...continued from page 11

might of the enemy must very soon be turned on us. Hitler knows that he will have to break us in this island or lose the war. If we can stand up to him, all Europe may be freed and the life of the world may move forward into broad, sunlit uplands. But if we fail, then the whole world, including the United States, including all that we have known and cared for, will sink into the abyss of a new Dark Age made more sinister, and perhaps more protracted, by the lights of perverted science. Let us therefore brace ourselves to our duty and so bear ourselves that, if the British Empire and its Commonwealth last for a thousand years, men will still say: 'This was their finest hour.'"

These were fine words, but privately Churchill believed that if the Germans landed Britain would hold out for no more than two weeks. However, for nearly a month after the fall of France, Hitler dallied, hoping that the British would settle. Then

on 16 July 1940, he signed Führer Directive No. authorizing Operation Sealion – the invasion England. The month had not been wasted by th British. They stepped up armament productio and prepared their defences.

On 19 July Hitler addressed the Reichstag, sayi that he saw no reason for further bloodshed an again, offered to come to terms with the Britis London made no response, so the preparations f Operation Sealion went ahead. The invasion wa set for 25 August.

The Germans had no specialized landing cra and began amassing fishing boats and rive barges to make the crossing. But there was problem. The invasion fleet would be vulnerabl to the Royal Navy, with the Royal Air Forc overhead. On land, over a million men ha signed up for the Local Defence Volunteer which, on 23 July, was renamed the Home Guard.

LEFT 'Walking wounded' British soldiers make their way up the gangplank from a destroyer at Dover on 31 May 1940.

ABOVE Destroyers filled with evacuated British troops berthing at Dover, 31 May 1940.

LEFT Adolf Hitler toured Paris and visited the Eiffel Tower on 28 June 1940, three days after the German armistice with France. Accompanying him were SS General Karl Wolff, Field Marshal Wilhelm Keitel, Hitler's chief adjutant SA-Obergruppenführer Wilhelm Bruckner, Reich Minister Albert Speer, Reich Leader Martin Borman, Secretary of State Otto Meissner and Press Secretary Otto Dietrich – architect Herman Giesler and sculptor Arno Breker were given field-grey uniforms for the occasion. Hitler also visited the Opera, the Madeleine, the Champs Elysées, the Panthéon, the Louvre, Montmartre and Les Invalides, where he stood for a long time beside Napoleon's tomb. However, he called off a parade that was in danger of being harassed by British air raids, saying: "I am not in the mood for a victory parade. We aren't at the end yet."

RIGHT Exhausted British troops rest on the quayside at Dover on 31 May 1940. They, too, knew that the war was not at an end yet.

...continued from page 15

To take control of the Channel and defen
the landing force, Germany would first hav
to command the air. German planes moved u
to airfields in Norway and Denmark, Belgiur
and Holland, and Northern France. Then on
August 1940, Hitler signed Führer Directive N
17, ordering the Luftwaffe to smash the RA
They were to bomb airfields, aircraft factorie
and factories producing anti-aircraft guns. The
were also to attack the ports which brough
in vital supplies – though leaving the Channe
ports intact as they would be needed in th
invasion. The Battle of Britain had begun.

LEFT Hitler and Admiral Erich Raeder in discussion at a map table
during a planning conference at the Berghof, July 1940. Also present
are (left to right): Army Commander-in-Chief Field Marshal Walther
von Brauchitsch, Chief of the Operations Staff General Alfred Jodl,
Head of Armed Forces (OKW) Field Marshal Wilhelm Keitel and an
unidentified Kriegsmarine staff officer.

COUNTDOWN

By August 1940 Germany had occupied northern France and signed an armistice with the new French government under Marshal Pétain at Vichy. Plans for the invasion of Britain were underway. Britain buckled down to preparing its defences and readying itself for the landings. Some voices still wanted to make peace with Hitler, but Churchill had already told the British people what they could expect. In the House of Commons on 4 June 1940 he said: "We shall fight on the beaches, we shall fight on the landing grounds, we shall fight in the fields and in the streets, we shall fight in the hills; we shall never surrender."

Everyone was expected to lend a hand. Men joined the Home Guard, whose members were largely too old or too young to be conscripted into the regular Army. They were to delay the enemy invasion force to give the Army time to form a proper defensive line. That in itself would be an almost impossible task as the Army had been forced to leave most of its heavy equipment in France.

Ill-equipped and at first armed only with privately-owned weapons, the Home Guard had a variety of tasks. They guarded bridges, tunnels, railway junctions and other transport infrastructure, they scouted for the Army and they manned road-blocks, the purpose of which was to capture enemy spies and paratroops. With these scant weapons, they were expected to fight and die.

However, the spirit was there. Head of the Home Guard training school at Osterley Park was Captain Tom Wintringham. A committed Marxist, he had seen action in the Spanish Civil War and compared the Home Guard to the International Brigade. And they knew what was expected of them. Churchill declared: "If all do their duty, if nothing is neglected, and if the best arrangements are made ... we shall prove ourselves once more able to defend our Island home, to ride out the storm of war, and to outlive the menace of tyranny, if necessary for years, if necessary alone."

Men of the Royal Navy's Coast Watch in a Lewis gun emplacement on the cliff top, watching for the approach of enemy aircraft.

LEFT Hermann Goering and staff view the white cliffs of Dover from the coast of France in the summer of 1940.

RIGHT An aerial photograph taken at 3,100 feet by a Bristol Blenheim of No. 82 Squadron RAF showing part of the docks at Dunkirk. Invasion barges are being assembled for Operation Sealion. These were vulnerable to attack. A number of sunk and damaged barges can be seen to the upper right. The wharves, roads and railway sidings are pitted with bomb craters, and two of the three warehouses on the central mole have been gutted.

RIGHT A German field gun crew practise for Operation Sealion - the invasion of Britain - on a beach in France.

ABOVE Concertina wire defences along the sea front at Sandgate, Kent, in July 1940. This would hardly have presented an obstacle to a dedicated landing force, but would have hampered pre-invasion scouts landed at night. Throughout the summer, Britain expected raiding parties to land by sea or air at any time.

ABOVE A pillbox on the promenade at the sea front at Worthing on 26 June 1940. The shallows would be mined and the beaches were off-limits to bathers.

RIGHT Royal Artillery gunners man a 6-inch coastal defence gun at Sheerness in November 1939. However, few shells are in evidence.

LEFT Lieutenant General Sir Ronald F. Adams, General Officer Commanding in Chief, makes a tour of inspection of some of the defences on the Northumbrian coast, accompanied by the area commander, Brigadier Hubert, in July 1924. General Adams and Brigadier Hubert are inspecting the barbed-wire defences of the 2nd/5th Battalion, Essex Regiment, 161st Brigade at Beadnell Bay.

RIGHT One of the units of the Royal Navy's Coast Watch. Teams of sailors were allocated to the defence of the coast and its military emplacements. They wore khaki Army battledress, but retained their Navy caps and leggings. The men are being paraded before taking up their positions.

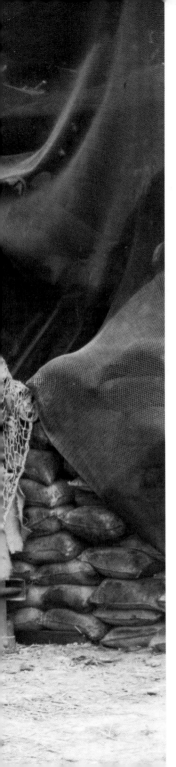

LEFT Winston Churchill inspecting 9.2-inch guns of 57th Heavy Regiment, Royal Artillery, during a tour of East Coast defences, 7 August 1940.

LEFT Women pilots, forming a section of the Air Transport Auxiliary (ATA) service, ferried new RAF aircraft from factory to aerodrome. This was dangerous work; often the aircraft had neither radios nor weapons, and if enemy aircraft were encountered, all they could do was open the throttle and head inland. 20 women died in service with the ATA. In this photograph the Commandant of the Women's Section of the ATA, Pauline Gower (far left), is seen with eight other founding female ATA pilots at Hatfield, Hertfordshire, by newly completed De Havilland Tiger Moths awaiting delivery to their pilot training units. The other pilots are (left to right): Winifred Crossley, Margaret Cunnison, Margaret Fairweather, Mona Friedlander, Joan Hughes, Gabrielle Patterson, Rosemary Rees and Marion Wilberforce.

ABOVE 'Pooh', one of two 14-inch guns emplaced at St Margaret's, near Dover. With its sister-gun, 'Winnie', it came from the reserve stock of guns for the 'King George V' class of battleships, and was mounted on modified naval barbettes.

RIGHT 'Winnie', named for the Prime Minister, was in place by August 1940 and 'Pooh' in February 1941. Manned by Royal Marine gunners, they were mostly employed in counter-battery fire with German batteries on the French coast.

LEFT Prime Minister Winston Churchill inspects the coastal defences near Grimsby. The big guns were reserved for the south coast, where the invasion was expected.

RIGHT A supply ship comes alongside one of the guardships protecting Plymouth. The guardship helped to guide British and Allied ships in to the port through the harbour defences - nets laced with explosives protected Plymouth against submarine attack.

LEFT Men of the Local Defence Volunteers – now renamed the Home Guard – line up for inspection. As Britain awaited invasion, none of them had a uniform beyond an LDV armband and none have weapons of any kind.

ABOVE A 4-inch mobile gun in position behind the sand dunes at Maplethorpe, Lincolnshire, on 30 July 1940. If the invasion force could not be held on the beaches, truck-mounted guns would provide vital mobile defence.

LEFT AND ABOVE Aluminium saucepans were collected to make Spitfires and other metal planes, while iron railings, old cannons and other scrap were melted down to make battleships. 'Saucepans for Spitfires' was one of the most famous wartime campaigns to encourage recycling. The official purpose of the campaign was to husband scarce resources, but even more vital was the boost it gave to the nation's morale by encouraging every citizen to contribute to the war effort.

ABOVE Spitfires being assembled at Eastleigh. They were tested by chief test pilot Jeffery Quill's team at the airfield there before being despatched to their squadrons.

RIGHT Prime Minister Winston Churchill watches a woman riveter working at an aircraft factory in Castle Bromwich, Birmingham. During World War II, 1,700,000 women between the ages of 20 and 30 were conscripted in Britain, releasing men for the armed forces.

FAR RIGHT Some 14,533 Hurricanes were built between 1936 and 1945. There was such a demand that Lord Beaverbrook, Minister of Aircraft Production in 1940, set up the Civilian Repair Organisation to recondition battle-damaged planes. He also put in new management to get the Spitfire production line in Castle Bromwich rolling.

LEFT Local defence volunteers practise on a make-shift rooftop shooting range on 24 June 1940.

ABOVE The Home Guard were trained in guerrilla warfare tactics at Osterley Park in Middlesex. Here a dummy tank, towed by a car, is disabled by a landmine in July 1940.

ABOVE Troops from the Grenadier Guards construct sandbag defences around government buildings in Birdcage Walk, London in May 1940.

RIGHT A team from the Royal Observer Corps look out for enemy planes on the roof of a suburban building in Eltham, southeast London.

ABOVE Here aircrew cadets are being given a lecture on navigation at No. 2 Initial Training Wing, Jesus College, Cambridge.

RIGHT Trainee pilots at No. 20 Service Flying Training School, Cranborne walk to Harvard Mark Is for their training flights. As war became inevitable, the Harvard (UK and Canadian designation for North American Aviation's AT-6 Texan) was ordered by the RAF to meet the massive increase in pilot training. This training station was in Southern Rhodesia (now Zimbabwe), part of an extensive Empire Air Training Scheme that saw airmen trained in the safety of distant lands for service in Britain.

LEFT Student pilots learn to identify vessels at sea using models on the Tactical Floor at No. 3 School of General Reconnaissance at Squires Gate, Blackpool, Lancashire.

ABOVE One of the key tasks of the Home Guard during the Battle of Britain was to guard crashed aircraft and take prisoner any German airmen who bailed out or survived a crash landing. Lessons in aircraft recognition were crucial for them. Here a group listens to a lecture by a Royal Artillery Sergeant on aircraft recognition in 1943, by which time big four-engined British bombers – such as the Stirling and Halifax to be seen here – were becoming an increasingly common sight in the skies over Britain.

THE MEN AND THEIR MACHINES

When the Battle of Britain began the RAF had three front-line fighters: the Boulton-Paul Defiant, the Hawker Hurricane and the Supermarine Spitfire. With its turret-mounted guns, the Defiant was designed to tackle bombers. The Hurricane was intended to tackle bombers or fighters. The iconic Spitfire was designed to defeat the Luftwaffe's fighters.

The Spitfire was the brain-child of aeronautical engineer Reginald Mitchell, who developed it from his series of record-breaking seaplanes. Both the Spitfire and the Hurricane used the Rolls Royce Merlin engine.

The Spitfires were made initially at Supermarine's main factories at Woolston and Itchen near Southampton but these were destroyed by an air raid on 26 September 1940. This was the Luftwaffe's second attempt to knock out these vital plants. Fortunately many of the production jigs and machine tools had already been removed as steps were being taken to disperse production across southern England. Parts were manufactured in small satellite workshops throughout the area and assembled at Eastleigh aerodrome. A second 'shadow' production line had been set up at Castle Bromwich in Birmingham.

During the Battle of Britain, the Hurricane accounted for more aircraft 'kills' than the Spitfire. It was designed by Hawker's chief designer Sydney Camm. His prototype first flew in 1935 and the first production models were delivered to the RAF in December 1937. The following year 200 had been delivered and the Gloster Aircraft company began producing them under licence to meet the demand. Before World War II, production began in Yugoslavia and Belgium, and, in 1940, they began being built in Canada.

The Defiant entered combat in May 1940. At first it performed well, destroying numerous enemy bombers. However, by that September the Germans had adopted new tactics and the Defiant was moved to a nightfighter role.

Although the popular image of a World War II RAF fighter pilot is of a young, upper class officer, this was not the case. Less than 8% had gone to public school, over 40% began their careers as sergeant pilots and 10% were over 30 years of age.

Six Supermarine Spitfire Mark Is of 19 Squadron RAF based at Duxford, Cambridgeshire, in 1938 flying in echelon formation led by the squadron commander, Squadron Leader H. I. Cozens. The squadron number on the tail plane was painted on shortly before the flight and removed afterwards. Fighter tactics evolved during the Battle of Britain. Eventually, all combatants adopted the *Schwarm* formation - known as 'Finger Four' by the British - developed by the Luftwaffe in the Spanish Civil War. The formation allowed aircraft to break into pairs to support each other during a dogfight.

During the Battle of Britain, Flight Lieutenant Adolph 'Sailor' Malan developed a new tactical formation for the 12-plane squadron, with four planes in a loose line astern following their three section leaders in a loose 'V'. This was easy for new pilots to fly while looking out for the enemy and broke into pairs offering mutual support. The three Supermarine Spitfire Mark Is shown, of 611 Squadron RAF, are flying in loose line astern over two other aircraft of the squadron at Digby, Lincolnshire.

ABOVE The RAF went into the Battle of Britain with three planes flying in 'V', 'Victory' or 'Vic' formations – sometimes with three or four 'Vics' forming a larger 'V' and a 'weaver' behind guarding the rear. This was abandoned as too rigid during the Battle of Britain. These Supermarine Spitfire Mark IAs – of 610 Squadron, based at Biggin Hill, Kent – fly in three 'Victory' formations.

ABOVE A Supermarine Spitfire Mark I of No 19 Squadron, Royal Air Force being rearmed between sorties at Fowlmere, Cambridgeshire.

RIGHT Flight Lieutenant Brendan 'Paddy' Finucane DFC, an Irishman who flew with the Royal Air Force, seated in the cockpit of his Supermarine Spitfire at RAF Kenley while serving with 452 Squadron.

LEFT Pilots of 19 Squadron RAF gather at Manor Farm, Fowlmere, after a sortie. Standing fourth from left is Squadron Leader B. J. E. 'Sandy' Lane, the Squadron CO. 19 were stationed variously at Duxford and Fowlmere.

LEFT Pilots of 19 Squadron relax between sorties outside their crew room at Manor Farm. They are (left to right), Pilot Officer W. Cunningham, Sub-Lieutenant A. G. Blake of the Fleet Air Arm (nicknamed The Admiral) and Flying Officer F. N. Brinsden, with Spaniel. Blake was killed the following month in a dogfight over Chelmsford, Essex.

Journalists of newspapers from the British Dominions watch a flight of Hawker Hurricane Mark Is from 56 Squadron RAF taking off for a sortie from North Weald, Essex. In the foreground another Hurricane Mark I of the Squadron stands at its dispersal point. Unlike the all-metal Spitfire, the Hurricane had a fabric-covered fuselage, which made it easier and cheaper to both manufacture and maintain.

ABOVE Free French trainee pilots prepare for take-off in Fairey trainers at the Franco-Belgian Air Training School, Odiham, Hampshire. A total of 276 Free French pilots were stationed in England after the fall of France and re-trained to fly in RAF squadrons.

ABOVE A Bristol Blenheim Mark IV of 40 Squadron RAF. After the fall of France Blenheim IVs began day and night attacks against German occupied ports and installations to disrupt the invasion plans. The Blenheim was the backbone of Britain's force of light bombers until 1942.

The Fairey Battle Mark I light bomber suffered very heavy losses leading up to the fall of France. Slow and poorly armed, the type proved no match for the Luftwaffe's fighters. After the return of the remaining Battles from France the RAF used the aircraft for cross-channel operations. Towards the end of 1940 all Battle squadrons were re-equipped with Wellingtons.

RIGHT An air-gunner of 264 Squadron RAF about to enter the gun turret of his Boulton Paul Defiant Mark I at Kirton-in-Lindsey, Lincolnshire. He is wearing the GQ Parasuit, supplied exclusively to Defiant gunners, which incorporates a parachute harness and life-saving jacket within a smock overall. There was not room in the turret for crew to wear a seat type or back-pack parachute.

ABOVE Surviving pilots of 601 Squadron RAF pose on a tractor used to negotiate the muddy conditions on the airfield at Exeter, Devon, in November 1940. 601 Squadron suffered crippling losses during the Battle of Britain and moved to Exeter on 7 September 1940 after being classified as overdue for rest and training of new pilots. Among the pilots identified are two flight commanders, Flight Lieutenant W P Clyde (first left) and Flying Officer T Grier (second left), who shot down nine and one shared, and eight and four shared, enemy aircraft respectively during the air battles over France and Britain.

ABOVE A Hawker Hurricane Mk I of 601 Squadron RAF being serviced in a dispersal at Exeter. The Hurricane was the first operational RAF aircraft to achieve speeds above 300mph. A total of 1715 Hurricanes flew with Fighter Command during the Battle of Britain. The aircraft's Rotol constant-speed propeller enabled the pilot to select optimum pitch for all modes of flight, from take-off to combat. The Hurricane was quicker to repair and rearm than the Spitfire, taking around ten minutes.

LEFT Fighter pilots of 610 Squadron (titled 'County of Chester') relax between sorties at Hawkinge. The Spitfire-equipped unit shot down 40 enemy aircraft during August 1940. It lost eleven pilots during the Battle of Britain. At this point in the war the 'Mae West' lifejacket was the only item of kit provided to keep downed fighter pilots afloat. They were also issued with dye to help the rescue services pick them out against the grey backdrop of the sea.

ABOVE Pilots and gunners of 264 Squadron pass the time with a game of draughts while waiting at 'readiness' outside their dispersal tent at Kirton-in-Lindsey, Lincolnshire. The first RAF squadron to be equipped with the two-seater Boulton Paul Defiant, it was at first successful but later suffered heavy losses until the shortcomings of the aircraft in daylight operations were recognized and it was converted to a nightfighter.

ABOVE Airmen holding down the tail of a Supermarine Spitfire Mark I of 611 Squadron RAF during a firing test of the wing-mounted guns at Digby, Lincolnshire, in January 1940. The early Mark I Spitfires had two-blade fixed-pitch wooden propellers. Later three- and four-blade propellers were used.

RIGHT Pilot Officer A. V. Taffy Clowes of No. I Squadron RAF, standing by the nose of his Hawker Hurricane Mark I at Wittering, Huntingdonshire. The wasp emblem was painted on the nose of his aircraft during the Battle of Britain, Clowes added a new stripe to the body for each enemy aircraft which he shot down. His final score was at least twelve.

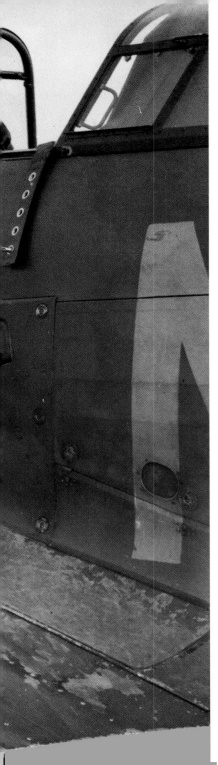

LEFT Armourers replenish the ammunition in a Hawker Hurricane Mark I of 310 (Czechoslovak) Squadron at Duxford, Cambridge, September 1940. There were two Czech squadrons in Fighter Command, 88 men in all. They shot down 60 aircraft for the loss of eight men.

BELOW Armourer Fred Roberts rearms a Spitfire Mark I of 19 Squadron at Fowlmere, while the pilot, Sergeant B. J. Jennings, has a word with his mechanic. Trust and respect were vital ingredients in the relationship between ground crew and pilots.

Czechoslovak pilots of 310 (Czechoslovak) Squadron RAF and their British flight commanders grouped in front of a Hawker Hurricane Mark I at Duxford, Cambridgeshire. They are (standing, left to right): Pilot Officer S. Janduch, Sergeant J. Vopalecuy, Sergeant R. Puda, Sergeant K. Seda, Sergeant B. Furst and Sergeant R. Zima: (sitting, left to right) Pilot Officer W. Goth, Flight Lieutenant J. Maly, Flight Lieutenant G. L. Sinclair, Flying Officer J. E. Boulton, Flight Lieutenant J. Jeffries (who commanded the Squadron in January-June 1941, having changed his name by deed poll to Latimer), Pilot Officer S. Zimprich, Sergeant J. Kaucky, Flight Lieutenant F. Rypl, Pilot Officer E. Fechtner and Pilot Officer V. Bergman. Formed at Duxford on 10 July 1940, and operational just a month later, 310 Squadron was the first RAF unit to be crewed by foreign personnel.

ABOVE A group of pilots from 303 (Polish) Squadron RAF stand by the tail elevator of one of their Hawker Hurricane Mark Is at Northolt, Middlesex. They are (left to right): Pilot Officer Miroslaw Feric, Flying Officers Bogdan Grzeszczak, Jan Zumbach and Zdzislaw Henneberg and Flight-Lieutenant J. A. Kent, who commanded the squadron's 'A' Flight at this time; October 1940. Only 80 per cent of the pilots who flew in the Battle of Britain were British citizens. The largest foreign contingent was Polish, with 145 airmen.

LEFT Sergeant B. Furst of 310 (Czechoslovak) Squadron RAF is greeted by the squadron mascot on returning to Duxford, Cambridgeshire, after a sortie in his Hawker Hurricane Mark I. Hurricane pilots were credited with four-fifths of all enemy aircraft destroyed in the period July–October 1940. For much of the Battle of Britain the principal targets of the Hurricanes were bomber formations flying at lower altitudes., leaving the Spitfires to deal with the speedier fighter escorts.

Formed from a cadre of experienced Czech fliers who had fled to England from their homeland, 310 Squadron claimed 37.5 victories during the Battle of Britain.

ABOVE Pilots of 310 (Czechoslovak) Squadron, based at Duxford, being debriefed by the Intelligence Officer after a sortie.

THE ENEMY ABOVE

Hitler's orders for the invasion of Britain gave the Luftwaffe explicit instructions: "The English air force must be beaten down to such an extent that it can no longer muster any power of attack worth mentioning against the German invasion fleet."

To achieve this aim, head of the Luftwaffe Hermann Goering (a former World War I fighter ace) assembled 2,442 front-line aircraft - 969 heavy bombers, 336 dive bombers, 869 single-engined fighters and 268 twin-engined fighters - plus a number of transports and reserve aircraft. They were stationed in captured airfields across northern France, the Low Countries, Denmark and Norway.

The best German fighter at this date was the Messerschmitt Bf 109, which was comparable to the RAF's Spitfire in performance and far more numerous. The longer range Bf 110 would prove to be less agile and vulnerable in combat, though still useful. Among the bombers the Heinkel III, Junkers Ju88 and Dornier Do17 all delivered heavy bomb loads over long distances, but were vulnerable unless escorted by fighters. The Junkers Ju87 Stuka divebomber delivered bombs with absolute precision, but only over shorter distances.

Throughout June and July, Goering sent small-scale raids over Britain to test the RAF defences, identify key targets and probe the mysterious radar systems. The Battle of Britain began in earnest on 8 August, with massed bombing raids on RAF bases, radar stations and other targets. These were intended not only to destroy the targets but also to lure up the RAF fighters so that they could be destroyed in air combat.

Unlike the RAF pilots, most of the aircrew in the Luftwaffe were professional airmen with years of training behind them. Many had already seen action and had developed effective tactics far superior to those of the RAF. Goering and his staff were confident they could carry out Hitler's orders.

A Messerschmitt Bf 110 flying over England, 1940. Known as 'Goering's folly', it was easy prey for the Hurricanes and Spitfires of the RAF because of its lack of agility.

LEFT A Messerschmitt Bf 109 of Fighter Wing 53 (JG 53) *Pik As* or 'Ace of Spades' (note the emblem on the removed engine cowling lying on the ground).

BELOW The leaders of the proposed invasion of Britain visit the bunker of advanced command post 'Caesar II' above Sangatte, near Calais. They are (left to right): Field Marshal Albert Kesselring, head of Luftflotte 2, with his Chief of Staff, Lieutenant General Wilhelm Speidel, and Reich Marshal Hermann Goering.

ABOVE Luftwaffe air crews study maps in the summer of 1940. In the background is a Dornier Do 17 light bomber.

RIGHT Hermann Goering addresses a group of German air crew during the Battle of Britain.

LEFT Luftwaffe ace Gunther Lützow wearing his Knight's Cross, which he was awarded in September 1940. In all he was credited with 110 victories in 300 combat missions. After the Battle of Britain his unit, JG 3, was sent to the Eastern Front, where Lützow fell foul of the SS for refusing to allow any of his men to be part of execution squads. He was a leading figure in the pilots' revolt which tried to get the dismissed Adolf Galland reinstated. Lützow went missing in combat, flying a Messerschmitt 262 jet fighter in an attack on a USAAF B-26 bomber, on 24 April 1945, two weeks before the war ended. Neither his body nor the aircraft was ever found.

RIGHT Adolf Galland was one of several highly-gifted aces put in charge of the Luftwaffe's fighter units by a dissatisfied Goering. He commanded JG 26, based in northern France, during the Battle of Britain. When asked by Goering how he would respond to an order to shoot enemy pilots in their parachutes, he said he would do all in his power to disobey. In 1941 he was made commander of Germany's fighter force, but was eventually sacked for his consistent criticism of the Nazi hierarchy's conduct of the air war.

RIGHT General Hans-Jürgen Stumpff, commander of Luftflotte 5, greets General Ernst Udet in front of Goering's hunting lodge Jägerhof Rominten. Stumpff and Udet helped rebuild the German air force in the 1930s after it was banned under the Treaty of Versailles. The highest scoring air ace to survive World War I, and one of the youngest (22), Udet had downed 62 enemy aircraft. At the outbreak of World War II, he was the Luftwaffe's Director-General of Equipment. When the supply of aircraft could not keep up with demand, he suffered a mental breakdown and committed suicide in November 1941.

FAR RIGHT Fighter ace Werner Mölders in conversation with head of the Luftwaffe, Hermann Goering, himself a fighter ace in World War I. During the Spanish Civil War, Mölders was instrumental in developing the four-aircraft 'Finger-four' formation, which proved to be far more effective in the Battle of Britain than the 'Vic' or 'Victory' close formation of three aircraft used by the RAF. Mölders shot down 29 British aircraft in the Battle of Britain. He had 101 victories to his name by the time of his death in a plane crash in 1941 when en route to Udet's funeral.

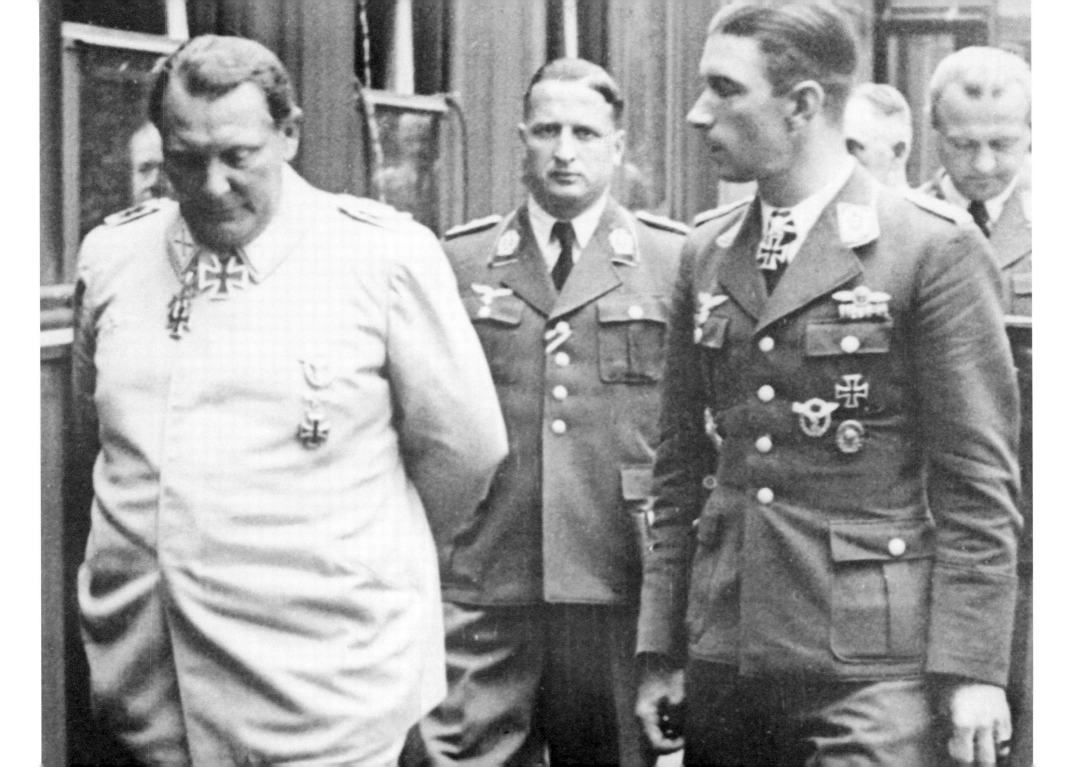

LEFT German Dornier 17Zs of II./KG77 being serviced on Freux auxiliary airfield in Belgium. This type was successful in the campaigns against Poland and France but subsequently suffered heavy losses over Britain during the autumn of 1940.

BELOW The Dornier Do17 was easy to catch but with its self-sealing fuel tanks plus radial engines that had no vulnerable cooling systems it could take a huge amount of punishment. The advantages of this bomber had been proved during the Spanish Civil War when Luftwaffe crews served as volunteers on the side of right-wing military leader General Franco. The experience gained by the crews proved to be invaluable and gave the Luftwaffe a crucial advantage over the Poles, French and others during the early months of the war.

ABOVE Junkers Ju 88 nightfighter, KBK LW 4. At low altitudes, it could nearly outrun a Spitfire.

RIGHT Ju 88s were manufactured at high volume. Some 313 Ju 88s were lost over Britain between July and October 1940.

ABOVE The Junkers Ju 88A-I – the original bomber version of the highly adaptable Junkers 88 aircraft.

LEFT German Heinkel He IIIs, which went into service in 1937 and soon became the Luftwaffe's principal bomber. Some 6,000 Heinkel He IIIs were built but, comparatively slow, under-armed and with poor manoeuvring capability, they were sitting targets for Hurricanes and Spitfires during the Battle of Britain. One asset was their ability to sustain considerable damage and remain airborne.

LEFT A Messerschmitt Bf 109 E-1 of 2nd Squadron of Fighter Wing (Jagdgeschwader) 20 being armed and serviced, ready for combat. The 109 could climb faster than a Spitfire, but had a lower rate of turn and its framed cockpit canopy offered poorer all-round visibility.

RIGHT The Messerschmitt Bf 109 was designed in the *Bayerische Flugzeugwerke* - Bavarian Aircraft Factory. The aircraft was later built or refitted by Erla Flugzeugwerke in Heiterblick, Abtnaundorf and Mockau. The Bf 109 went into service in 1937. The plane's gentle stall could be used to advantage in a dogfight.

LEFT Heinkel He III bombers attack in formation. A hundred miles an hour slower than the Spitfire, they were an easy target and left to the slower Hurricanes.

BELOW The Junkers Ju-87 Stuka dive-bomber delivered bombs with pinpoint accuracy, but proved vulnerable to attack by fighter aircraft.

RIGHT A Heinkel He III bomber flying over Wapping and the Isle of Dogs in the East End of London at the start of the Luftwaffe's evening raids of 7 September 1940. This attack signalled a shift in Hitler's thinking and in the course of the campaign, with the focus moving from military targets to the civilian population. For the next 57 days, London would be bombed..

A Messerschmitt Bf 109 E of JG 2 'Richthofen' KBK LW5 taxiing in October 1940. The E, or 'Emil', version used in the Battle of Britain had heavier armament, increased fuel capacity and the more powerful 1,100 PS Daimler-Benz DB 601 engine that increased its top speed by 60mph. The use of fuel injection rather than a carburettor delivered better performance in negative 'g' force than the Spitfire or Hurricane, giving the 109 better diving ability in a dogfight.

ABOVE Major John Schalk John and Lieutenant Theodor Rossiwal (right) of Zerstorer ('Destroyer') Squadron 26 in front of Bf 110 PK KBK LW 3 in the summer of 1940. Schalk claimed six victories during the Battle of Britain; three of them were shot down by his backseat wireless operator/gunner. He was awarded the Iron Cross on 5 September 1940.

LEFT The cockpit of a Messerschmitt Bf 110, viewed from behind the dashboard of the radio operator/rear gunner; November 1940. The Bf 110 was designed as an escort fighter and did not live up to expectations during the Battle of Britain.

A formation of Dornier Do 17 Z KBK LW 3C
on a mission over England in 1940.

ABOVE Heinkel He 59 seaplanes were used for air-sea rescue during the Battle of Britain. Suspecting that they were in fact radioing information to German bombers to help them reach their targets, the RAF shot a number of them down. After this the aircraft were repainted in their original military colour schemes.

COMMAND AND CONTROL

Since 1938, the British had developed the most advanced radar defence network in the world, stretching from Land's End to the Shetland Islands. Incoming German planes could be detected in time for commanders to get their fighters airborne, so they were not caught and destroyed on the ground. Control centres fed with radar information could direct the fighters by radio to intercept the enemy aircraft, though later in the Battle the Germans learned how to evade interception.

The head of Fighter Command, Air Chief Marshal Sir Hugh Dowding, had encouraged the development of radar. He also devised the 'Dowding system', which co-ordinated the information coming in from radar stations and observers about incoming enemy formations on a map table. Commanders could then assess the situation and send out their orders to the fighters. The whole network was tied together by dedicated phone links buried sufficiently deep to protect them against bomb damage.

The network had its apex at RAF Bentley Priory, a converted country house on the outskirts of London which also served as Dowding's headquarters. The system sometimes worked brilliantly, often allowing the RAF to break up or shoot down enemy formations before they reached their targets.

The RAF had another advantage. The Battle was being fought over home soil, enabling the British to recover their downed pilots. If a German aircraft was shot down both the plane and the crew were lost. On 15 August 1940, for example, while 70 German planes were shot down, 28 Hurricanes and Spitfire were also lost, but half of their pilots eventually returned to their squadrons. This was vital because throughout the Battle of Britain the RAF suffered from a shortage of trained pilots.

Pilots of No 87 Squadron run to their Hurricane fighters for a practice 'scramble' at Lille-Seclin in northern France in November 1939. By then some replacement Hurricanes were arriving in France fitted with the de Havilland three-bladed variable-pitch propeller, as shown here.

LEFT King George VI and Queen Elizabeth visit the Headquarters of Fighter Command at Bentley Priory, near Stanmore, Middlesex. They are escorted by Air Chief Marshal Sir Hugh Dowding, Air Officer Commander-in-Chief of Fighter Command.

ABOVE An aerial view of RAF Bentley Priory, Stanmore, Middlesex, the Headquarters of Fighter Command, seen from the south-west.

LEFT After the Second World War, Lord Tedder, Chief of the Air Staff, would state: "If any one man won the Battle of Britain, he did. I do not believe it is realized how much that one man, with his leadership, his calm judgment and his skill, did to save, not only this country, but the world."

The man in question was Air Vice-Marshal Keith Park, who commanded 11 Group, responsible for defending London and the south-east against the Luftwaffe during the Battle of Britain. The New Zealand-born Park used to fly a personalized Hurricane to visit the fighter squadrons under his command. He is seen here getting in to the cockpit of his aircraft.

RIGHT Meanwhile 12 Group, under the command of Air Vice Marshal Trafford Leigh-Mallory, was deployed to defend the airfields; he is seen inspecting members of the WAAF (Women's Auxiliary Air Force) at a Fighter Command station. The two men fell out over tactics. Park used single squadrons in hit-and-run attacks on the enemy. Leigh-Mallory favoured the 'Big Wing' of three to five squadrons acting together. Both approaches had their virtues. Park's single-squadron tactic was flexible and responsive, while 12 Group, stationed further to the north, had more time to get their planes in to formation.

Fighter Command's commanding officer, Air Chief Marshal Sir Hugh Dowding, did nothing to resolve the conflict. At the end of the Battle of Britain, both Dowding and Park were removed from their posts, and Leigh-Mallory was given command of 11 Group.

LEFT The pilots of 615 Squadron
are briefed before they take off
to face the enemy.

ABOVE Two RAF Battle of Britain pilots in 1940. They are already wearing
their headphones and microphones so they can plug into their planes' radio
telephones as soon as they are scrambled.

LEFT Prime Minister Winston Churchill at his desk in the Map Room. Beside him is Captain Pym of the Royal Navy Volunteer Reserve. The purpose of the Map Room was to provide Churchill with a snapshot of the progress of the war and so inform his strategic decision-making. The Room was part of the The Cabinet War Rooms complex set up by Churchill to ensure there were clear lines of communication between the policy makers and the military. Decisions taken in the Cabinet Room were passed for implementation to senior officers of all three armed services working together in the Map Room. Some 2000 people worked in the Cabinet War Rooms (also called Storey's Gate), which were located beneath the Treasury Building in Whitehall.

RIGHT Dowding masterminded the development of a radar-assisted control system from the Operations Room at Bentley Priory. Under the Dowding system, the WAAFs moved blocks representing enemy aircraft across the map table. Commanders viewed from above and issued appropriate orders to interceptors. Their movements were also mapped on the table. This photograph shows the original control centre located in the ballroom at Bentley Priory where Dowding experimented with table layouts, where personnel should stand or sit and other features of the control room. Once the layout was finalized, late in 1939, the control room was moved to a purpose-built underground bunker outside the house where it would be safe from German bombing raids.

LEFT A Sound Locator on a tripod mounting in operation with an anti-aircraft battery.

BELOW A Mobile Sound Locator of the 1st Anti-Aircraft Division, Territorial Army Mobile Display Group, in use at night.

These photographs were widely publicized in 1939 and 1940 in an attempt to hide the introduction of radar.

RIGHT Air bases came under sustained attack from the Luftwaffe during the Battle of Britain. Armoured trucks such as these, at Wyton, Cambridgeshire, might have been effective against a land force, but could do nothing to combat attacks from the air. They were intended for use against paratroops who were expected to form the first wave of a German invasion.

LEFT Chain Home was the code name for the ring of early warning radar stations built before the war. This one was at Ventnor on the Isle of Wight. The airmen and WAAF operators manning the receiver hut played a vital role in the Battle of Britain.

BELOW The radar receiver towers and bunkers at Woody Bay near St Lawrence on the Isle of Wight were a 'Remote Reserve' station to receiver room at Ventnor and were part of the Chain Home system.

RIGHT Interior of a receiver room at an AMES Type 2 CHL station – CHL or Chain Home Low was a late development used to spot low-flying aircraft that was first demonstrated in July 1939. On the right are the Plan Position Indicator (PPI) radar display and the Range console, and in the centre is the Air Plotting Board.

BELOW Two Dornier 17 bombers over West Ham, London. They had already made their way through the coastal anti-aircraft gunnery screen and past the interceptors.

RIGHT Interior of a receiver room at an AMES Type 2 CHL station – CHL or Chain Home Low was a late development used to spot low-flying aircraft that was first demonstrated in July 1939. On the right are the Plan Position Indicator (PPI) radar display and the Range console, and in the centre is the Air Plotting Board.

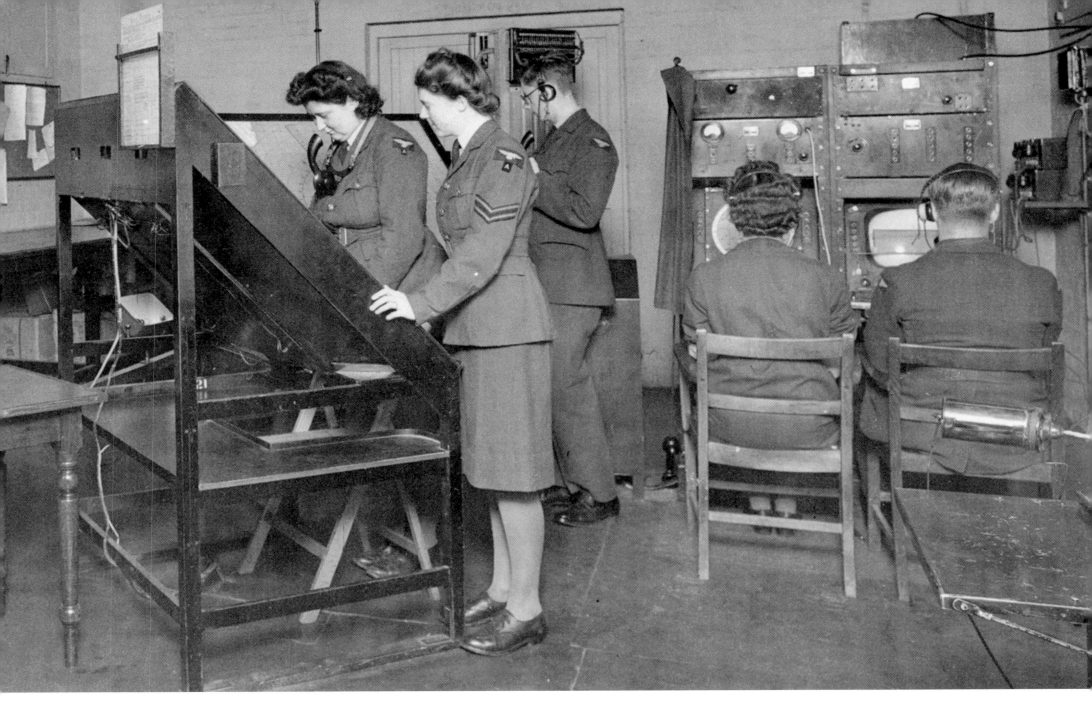

RIGHT An aerial view of Croydon, Surrey, seen from the south-west. RAF Croydon – formerly London's international airport – was home to eight squadrons during the Battle of Britain. Close to London, it was regularly bombed.

LEFT Interior of the Sector 'G' Operations Room at Duxford, Cambridgeshire. The callsigns of fighter squadrons controlled by this Sector can be seen on the wall behind the operator sitting third from left. The Controller is sitting fifth from the left, and on the extreme right, behind the Army Liaison Officer, are the radio-telephone operators in direct touch with the aircraft.

BELOW A Boulton Paul Defiant Mark I nightfighter of 264 Squadron RAF, is silhouetted against the clouds while making a low-level pass over its base at Biggin Hill in Kent.

RIGHT Trailing black smoke, a British RAF fighter plane goes down over England in December 1940.

ABOVE During the first phase of the Battle of Britain, when RAF airfields were among the Luftwaffe's principal targets, those on watch were as likely to be looking out for enemy aircraft as their own fighters. Air strikes against them were sometimes so sudden that they preceded the sounding of air raid sirens.

RIGHT A British RAF Hawker Hurricane aircraft has its wing torn off by a German fighter plane during a dogfight over England in November 1940.

LEFT The RAF-run Air Sea Rescue Service operated both seaplanes and high-speed launches. Two Type 2 'Whaleback' HSLs are shown here. The low-profile cabin contained a wheel-house, chart room and a sick bay. The two aircraft-style turrets were each equipped with a single .303 Vickers machine-gun. Over 200 airmen were killed or went missing in the waters around the British Isles during the Battle of Britain.

THE FEW

On 20 August 1940, Prime Minister Winston Churchill told a packed House of Commons of the valiant struggle of RAF Fighter Command to hold the Luftwaffe at bay.

He said: "The gratitude of every home in our Island, in our Empire, and indeed throughout the world, except in the abodes of the guilty, goes out to the British airmen who, undaunted by odds, unwearied in their constant challenge and mortal danger, are turning the tide of the world war by their prowess and by their devotion. Never in the field of human conflict has so much been owed by so many to so few."

That last resonating sentence had come to Churchill on 16 August while he was travelling back from visiting RAF Uxbridge, the Headquarters of II Group.

After the speech, the RAF fighter pilots became known, proudly, as 'The Few'. There were fewer than three thousand of them, of whom 510 were killed. Most were British. Others came from the Dominions – Australia, Canada, New Zealand and South Africa. Several squadrons were made up of Poles, Czechs and Belgians who had escaped from occupied Europe. Smaller numbers came from France, Ireland and the US. They faced enormous odds and, at the height of the Battle of Britain, they went into action several times a day.

For two weeks after Churchill's speech the Germans concentrated on bombing Fighter Command airfields. Several were knocked out for some days and othes were severely damaged. And 'The Few' became fewer as casualties rose alarmingly. Dowding had to borrow bomber pilots to keep his fighter aircraft flying. By 28 August the situation was so dire that trainee pilots with as little as nine hours' experience in fighters were sent up. The RAF were losing the Battle .

RAF Spitfires patrol the British coast.

LEFT Ground crew refuel Hawker Hurricane Mark Is of III Squadron RAF at Wick, Caithness. They were sent north to guard the Royal Navy in Scapa Flow. The relationship between pilots and ground crew was close, with individual crews looking after specific aircraft and pilots. Ground crew would work tirelessly to patch up aircraft and make sure they were ready for the next day's combat.

RIGHT South African ace Albert 'Zulu' Lewis returns from a sortie in his Hawker Hurricane during the Battle of Britain. Many pilots returned to base after combat completely exhausted and had to be helped out of the cockpit. It was not unusual for fighter pilots to fly four or five sorties a day. On 27 September 1940 Lewis shot down 6 aircraft in one day.

LEFT Pilot Officer William Lidstone 'Willie' McKnight, a fighter pilot from Calgary, Canada, served with 242 (Canadian) Squadron RAF during the Battle of Britain and was the first Canadian air ace of the war. Between May and November 1940, he claimed 16.5 victories in combat over France and England. He was shot down and killed during a low level sortie over France on 12 January 1941.

RIGHT A group of pilots of 1 Squadron RCAF gather round one of their Hawker Hurricane Mark Is at Prestwick, Scotland. The Squadron Commanding Officer, Squadron Leader E. A. McNab, stands fifth from the right, wearing a forage cap. McNab brought the squadron over from Canada in June 1940. Once it was operational, he shot down 6 enemy aircraft. He was awarded the DFC in October 1940 and returned to Canada the following month. In March 1941, 1 Squadron RCAF was renumbered 401 Squadron in line with the policy to eliminate the duplication of numbering among RAF and non-RAF units.

LEFT Still from gun camera film shot by Flight Lieutenant A.G. 'Sailor' Malan, leader of 'A' Flight, 74 Squadron RAF, recording his first aerial victory, a Heinkel He III over Dunkirk. Although debris and billowing smoke issue from the Heinkel's starboard engine and the starboard undercarriage has dropped, Malan's claim was categorized as unconfirmed since he did not observe the aircraft's destruction. 'A' Flight was based at Hornchurch but was flying out of Rochford at this time in order to shorten the patrol range to France. By the end of July 1941, South African Malan had achieved a total of 27 and seven shared confirmed victories, and two and one shared unconfirmed victories to become the highest scoring pilot of the war in Fighter Command.

ABOVE Hurricane Mk I of Squadron Leader Robert Stanford Tuck, commanding 257 Squadron, refuelling at Coltishall, early January 1941. The Squadron was based at RAF Northolt during the Battle of Britain.

RIGHT Group Captain A.G. 'Sailor' Malan climbing in to the cockpit of his Supermarine Spitfire at Tangmere, Sussex while commanding No. 145 Wing based at Manston.

LEFT Squadron Leader Stanford Tuck poses with a group of pilots of 257 Squadron, RAF under the nose of a Hawker Hurricane at Martlesham Heath, Suffolk. They are displaying souvenirs of their action against Italian aircraft on 11 November 1940, when 14 enemy aircraft were shot down and many more were damaged. The port of Harwich had been the target of the raid, which was the last attempted by the Italian Air Force against Britain. Morale in the squadron was very low when Tuck took over, but he turned it into one of the best fighter units in the RAF Tuck himself went on to become one the highest scoring British air aces, accounting for at least 27 enemy aircraft in the Battle of Britain. In 1942 he was captured by German forces after his Spitfire was damaged by ground fire. Shortly after his capture, he was invited to dinner by air ace Adolf Galland. He was moved to the Luftwaffe-run Stalag Luft III POW camp in Silesia, where he was involved in several escape attempts, finally succeeding in February 1945.

RIGHT A long-standing injury prevented one of the RAF's most celebrated air aces from participating in the Batttle of Britain. Wing Commander J.E. Johnson was the highest scoring RAF pilot to survive the war, with 38 'kills'. Remarkably, he was never shot down. Johnson gained invaluable tactical experience flying as Douglas Bader's No. 2 in 616 Squadron in 1941. He is seen here when he was leader of No. 144 (Canadian) Wing RAF, resting on the wing of his Spitfire Mark IX between sorties with his Labrador retriever Sally.

LEFT After an awards ceremony at Hornchurch, Essex, decorated RAF pilots cheer King George VI. They are (left to right): Flying Officer J. L. Allen, Flight-Lieutenant R. R. Stanford Tuck, Flight-Lieutenant A. C. Deere, Flight-Lieutenant A. G. Malan, Squadron-Leader J. A. Leathart and an airman bugler. Allen, Deere, and Leathart, all serving with 54 Squadron RAF, had, between them, shot down 25 enemy aircraft by the end of the Battle of France.

RIGHT Pilots of 43 Squadron RAF based at Wick, Caithness, in front of one of the unit's Hawker Hurricanes, shortly before moving south to take part in the Battle of Britain. They are (left to right): Sergeants J Arbuthnot, R. Plenderleith and H. J. L. Hallows, Flying Officer J. W. Simpson, Flight Lieutenant P. W. Townsend (who would later be involved in a romance with Princess Margaret) and Pilot Officer H. C. Upton.

LEFT Squadron Leader Douglas Bader (front centre) with some of the pilots of his 242 (Canadian) Squadron, grouped around his Hurricane at Duxford. They are (left to right): Dennis Crowley-Milling, Hugh Tamblyn (killed in action, 3 April 1941), Stan Turner, J.E. Savill, Neil Campbell (killed in action, 17 October 1940), Willy McKnight (killed in action, 12 January 1941), Bader, G.E. Ball (killed in action, date unknown), M.G. Homer (killed in action, 27 September 1940) and Ben Brown (killed in flying accident, 21 February 1941).

Morale was low when Bader took command of 242 Squadron. Heavy losses suffered during the battle for France had taken their toll. There were suspicions, too, that Bader would be a desk-bound commander when what they needed was a leader; Bader had lost both legs in a flying accident in 1931. But he soon won them over, proving his prowess as a pilot and as an administrator who did not mind upsetting his superiors if it meant his squadron received the spares and equipment it needed to operate effectively.

RIGHT Bader was a leading advocate of the 'Big Wing' concept, which involved RAF squadrons deploying in numbers to intercept and destroy the German bombers and their escorts that were attacking Britain daily.

BELOW Rene Mouchotte (second from right) was the first Frenchman to command
an RAF squadron and one of 12 French airmen who fought in the Battle of Britain.
Extreme left in this photograph is Lieutenant Duperier, who took over command
of 341 Squadron (Groupe Chasse 'Alsace') after Mouchotte's death in September
1943. Writing in his log after his 140th sortie (he would fly 382 missions in all),
Mouchotte noted: "My fatigue is merciless and I feel my nerves breaking. I have
an unbearable need of rest. I haven't taken a week's leave in over two years."

LEFT Australian pilots of the recently
formed 452 Squadron, photographed at
Kirton-in-Lindsey, 18 June 1941. It was
the first Australian squadron to form
in Britain during the Second World War
and one of the most successful units in
Fighter Command. During just 13 months
in Britain the squadron shot down over
62 enemy aircraft and damaged a further
17, for the loss of 22 pilots. One of its most
unusual missions was to drop an artificial
leg for Douglas Bader, who was then a
prisoner-of-war in France. The squadron
returned home in June 1942 to take part
in the war in the Pacific.

LEFT RAF fighter pilots in their makeshift mess area. Many airfields had been built quickly with few facilities and men had to be in their flying gear at all times, ready to fly at a moment's notice.

LEFT British pilots scramble to their aircraft. This could happen four or five times a day.

BELOW A section of three Hawker Hurricane Mark Is of 257 Squadron RAF take off from snow-bound Coltishall, Norfolk. They are led by the Squadron's Commanding Officer, Squadron Leader R. R. Stanford Tuck, in V6864 DT-A.

ABOVE A still from camera gun footage taken from a Supermarine Spitfire Mark I of 609 Squadron RAF flown by Pilot Officer R.F.G. Miller, showing a Heinkel He III of KG 53 or KG 55 taking hits in the port engine from Miller's machine guns. The aircraft was one of a force which bombed the Bristol Aeroplane Company's factory at Filton, Bristol. Miller was killed two days later when his aircraft collided head on with a Messerschmitt Bf 110 of III/ZG 26 over Cheselbourne, Dorset.

RIGHT A crashed Heinkel He IIIP, IG+NT, of III/KG27, shot down by Blue Section of 92 Squadron RAF at 6 pm on 14 August 1940, lying by the side of the road at Charterhouse, Somerset. Note the machine gun projecting from the starboard side of the fuselage as protection from beam attacks.

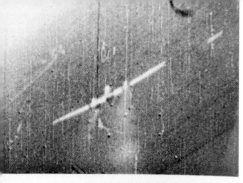
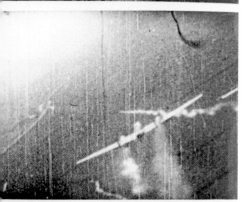

LEFT Sequence of camera gun still frames showing the destruction of a Bf 110 by a British fighter.

ABOVE Hawker Hurricanes of 85 Squadron RAF in battle formation.

LEFT A still from camera gun footage taken by a Supermarine Spitfire Mark I of 609 Squadron RAF, flown by Pilot Officer M.E. Staples, showing a Messerschmitt Bf 110 banking steeply to port as it tries to avoid Staples' gun fire. This aircraft belongs either to Erprobungsgruppe 210, which bombed the Parnall aircraft factory at Yate, north-east of Bristol, or to III/ZG 76 which was providing fighter cover for Heinkel He IIIs of KG 55 as they attempted to attack the Bristol Aeroplane Company's factory at Filton.

BELOW The wreckage of a Messerschmitt Bf 110 fighter bomber which crashed after a raid on Croydon in August 1940.

THEIR FINEST HOUR

On 18 June 1940 - just six and a half weeks after taking over as Prime Minister - Winston Churchill told the House of Commons that the Battle of France was over and the Battle of Britain was about to begin. He warned of the consequences of failure, not just for Britain, but the whole world. He had already warned the people of Britain that all he had to offer them was "blood, toil, tears and sweat". The British people were now to brace themselves to their duties and so bear themselves, "that if the British Empire and its Commonwealth last for a thousand years, men will still say, 'This was their finest hour' ".

On 23 August a force of Heinkel III bombers accidentally bombed part of London. In retaliation the RAF sent 81 bombers to Berlin two nights later. Hitler was furious, declaring "they have attacked our cities, so we shall wipe out theirs".

Many of Goering's senior officers had always doubted that the German navy would be able to transport their army across the Channel. They had advocated a campaign of bombing Britain's industrial cities to destroy the country's ability to wage war. Now they had their chance - the Blitz began.

The switch by the Luftwaffe from attacking RAF targets to bombing Britain's cities only served to stiffen the nation's collective resolve not to give in. The armed forces and the citizenry were united in the war against Nazism. In addition to the formal mobilization of civilians into recognized units, such as the Home Guard and the Land Army, the public at large willingly became part of the war effort, not least by accepting the necessary deprivations with stoicism and good humour. Britain would not negotiate with 'that man' - Hitler - nor would it let him invade without putting up a fight. The battle lines had been drawn and there was only one side to be on.

Churchill, as always, judged the public mood perfectly. He had already told his Cabinet colleagues: "I am convinced that every man of you would rise up and tear me down from my place if I were for one moment to contemplate parley or surrender. If this long island story of ours is to end at last, let it end only when each of us lies choking in his own blood upon the ground."

Communication was a vital component of the Battle of Britain. For Fighter Command to parry the Luftwaffe, information from observers and radar stations had to reach the operations room, then orders had to get through to the airfields.

RIGHT Air Raid Precautions dog Rip searches amongst brick rubble, timber and papers for survivors after an air raid in Poplar, London, 1941. Picked up as a stray by an ARP warden, Rip became one of eight dogs on the Home Front to win the Dickin Medal for bravery; named after Maria Dickin, the founder of the People's Dispensary for Sick Animals, the medal is known as the animals' Victoria Cross. His headstone reads: "Rip, D.M., 'We also serve', for the dog whose body lies here played his part in the Battle of Britain."

ABOVE An Air Raid Precautions messenger boy, thought to be on St Mary's in the Scilly Isles. He is wearing a steel helmet with the letter 'M' stuck on it. His 'ARP' badge is clearly visible on his lapel.

RIGHT An Air Raid Warden wearing gas protective clothing, gas mask and steel helmet. The gas protection outfit is an oilskin overall, similar in style to Churchill's famous one-piece 'siren suit'.

LEFT An anti-aircraft searchlight and crew in the grounds of the Royal Hospital at Chelsea in London on 17 April 1940.

RIGHT Anti-aircraft gun emplacements were set up in many of London's parks to help protect the city against the Luftwaffe's bombing raids. Here a range finder and predictor sited in Primrose Hill are shown. In the top right of the picture a 4.5 inch gun can be seen.

LEFT A member of the Women's Land Army is trained in the traditional horse-drawn method of ploughing at the WLA training centre at Cannington in Somerset, *c.* 1940. First created in the First World War the WLA was re-formed in June 1939. It remained in existence until its disbandment in 1950. Food rationing would last a further four years.

RIGHT The blockade on Britain led to shortages in food as well as raw materials. The pressure was so great that even public parks were turned into allotments and the public was urged to 'Dig for Victory and provide their own food'. This woman waters the vegetables on her allotment in Kensington Gardens with the help of a Westminster Civil Defence Warden .

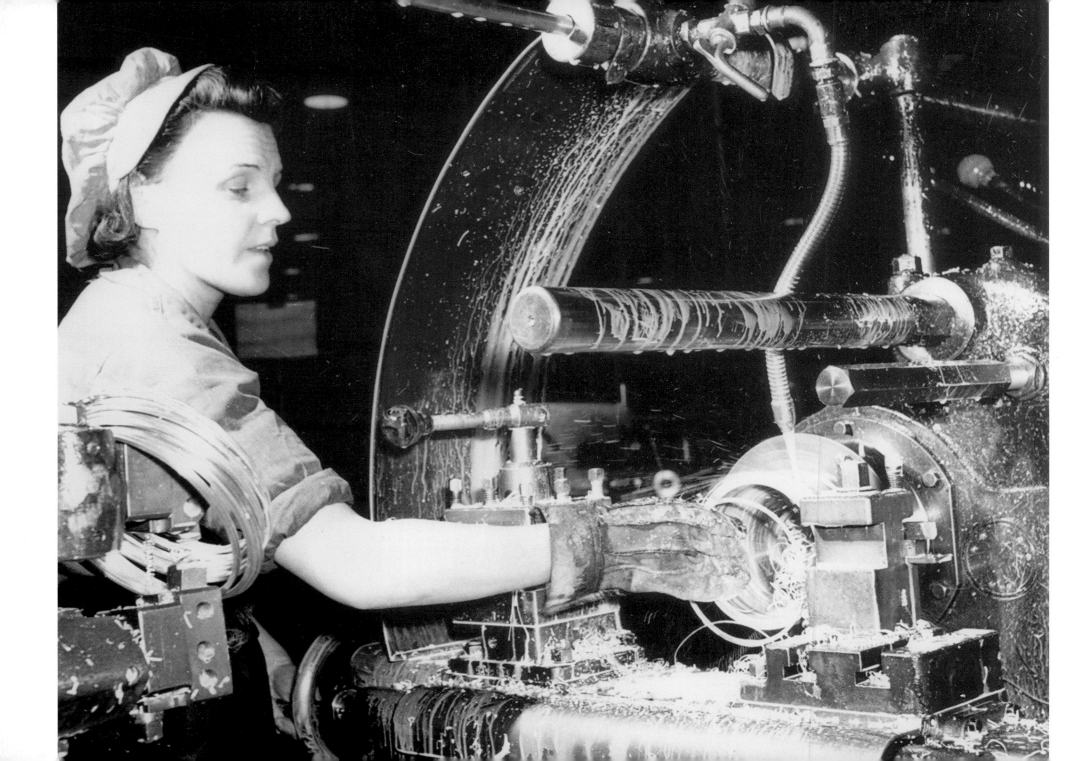

LEFT Mary Gordon operates a No 7 Ward combination lathe, producing sealing rings for the cylinder at this aircraft engine factory at a secret location. This was precision work, as an error of 0.001 inch would lead to the seizing up of the entire engine.

RIGHT A London postman on his delivery round in the aftermath of a bombing raid. Whole streets could be obliterated overnight, completely altering the cityscape. Post office workers were themselves vulnerable to attack, as the Luftwaffe targeted communication centres such as post offices.

ABOVE Firemen directing hoses on burning buildings in the city of Manchester after an air raid.

RIGHT A building gutted by an incendiary bomb in Manchester after a German air raid.

LEFT In 1939 the Café de Paris in Piccadilly was allowed to stay open even though London's West End theatres and cinemas were closed by order. The maître d' Martin Poulson argued that the four storeys of solid masonry above the club provided ample protection. He was proved tragically wrong - on 8 March 1941 two landmines came through the Rialto roof and exploded on the Café's dance floor. Eighty people were killed, including Ken 'Snakehips' Johnston who was performing on stage at the time and Poulson himself.

RIGHT Thames water-tenders and fire-boats attempt to put out fires in warehouses at Southwark Reach in 1940.

LEFT Doris and Alan Suter step down into the Anderson shelter in the garden of their home at 44 Edgeworth Road, Eltham in London in the summer of 1940. Their mother, Mrs Suter, can just be seen behind them outside the shelter. Alan is carrying his gas mask in its box with him.

RIGHT An Anderson shelter remains intact amidst destruction and debris, after a land mine fell a few yards away. The three people that had been inside the shelter were not hurt. The effects of air raids in this area of London can be clearly seen behind the shelter. This photograph was taken on Latham Street in Poplar.

RIGHT A row of terraced houses in Gosport, Hampshire after a raid of 12 August 1940. Those nearest the cameraman have been badly damaged and a pile of rubble is in the street.

LEFT & RIGHT On 10 October 1940 a bomb hit St Paul's Cathedral in London, wrecking the altar and damaging the roof. However, amidst the devastation of the City of London, St Paul's remained standing and became a symbol of defiance.

LEFT On the night of 29 December German aircraft attacked the City of London with incendiaries and high-explosive bombs, causing a conflagration that has been called the Second Great Fire of London. Among the buildings damaged that night was the Guildhall, which lost its roof. Another raid five months later left the whole building wrecked. Many of the Guildhall's treasures had been transferred to the countryside for storage at the start of the war but a number of paintings and heavier objects remained and were lost forever.

RIGHT A fiireman regards the ruins of Gieves & Hawkes, the naval and military tailors, in London's Old Bond Street, which had taken a direct hit after a bombing raid on 16 September 1940.

LEFT The King and Queen stand amid the bomb damage at Buckingham Palace. The Palace was a deliberate target for the Luftwaffe as the German High Command felt that its destruction would demoralize the nation. It had the opposite effect. The Queen was famously to utter, "I'm glad we have been bombed. Now I can look the East End in the face."

ABOVE After another night of German bombing in September 1940, three children sit next to the remains of their home in East London. Having failed to destroy the RAF, the Luftwaffe turned their attention to bombing Britain's cities in the Blitz.

ABOVE Shoppers look for Christmas gifts at London's Petticoat Lane market on 8 December 1940.
People still came to the street market even though many shops had been bombed out in the Blitz.

BELOW Women and children queue past several shops to buy goods from 'Patsy' the greengrocer on a shopping street in London. Also clearly visible are the signs of the Victoria Wine Co. Ltd. and Stevens and Steed. Outside, in the bottom right hand corner of the photograph, are two bicycles carrying a sign that reads 'Gunther Jolly Good Butcher'.

RIGHT A grocer's shop with goods piled high on the counter. Egg substitutes and mixes requiring no eggs are much in evidence. Under rationing an adult was allowed one egg a week or one packet of egg powder - making the equivalent of twelve eggs - a month.

LEFT A panoramic view of the city of Liverpool, showing bomb damage received after an air raid. The Liver Building can be clearly seen just to the right of centre, and the River Mersey is just visible in the left of the photograph.

ABOVE More bomb damage to Liverpool. Admiral Karl Dönitz persuaded Hitler to concentrate the Luftwaffe's bombing campaign on the ports to support his U-boat campaign in the Battle of the Atlantic and prevent supplies coming in from North America.

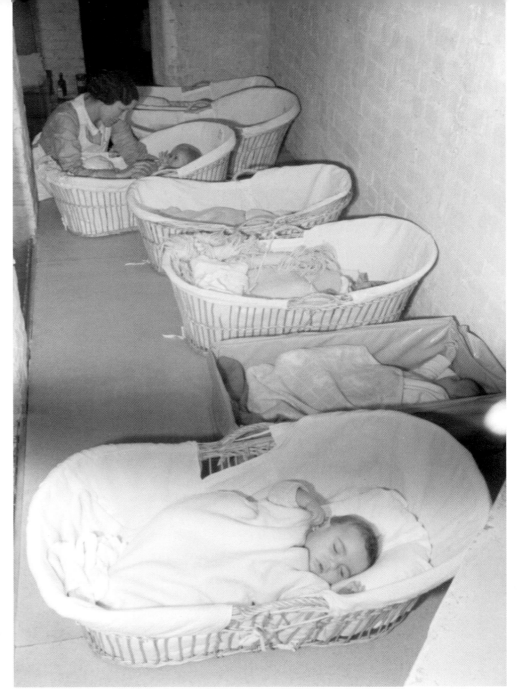

ABOVE Four women and a man sit in their 'refuge room', using their Morrison shelter as a table. They have covered the shelter with a table cloth and are enjoying a spot of afternoon tea.

RIGHT Babies sleep in their baskets in the air raid shelter of the 'Foster Parents Plan for War Children' Nursery in Hampstead, London in 1941. The shelter appears to be in the basement of the nursery.

LEFT A couple asleep in a prototype indoor shelter. It was similar to a Morrison shelter, but had a rounded, corrugated metal roof, rather than the flat, steel table-top of the Morrison type. This shelter gave the occupants more headroom, but was found to be less practical around the home than the flat-topped Morrison.

LEFT The curate of John Keble Church in Mill Hill, north London, tends to one of the many people taking shelter in the nave of the church in 1940. Many homeless and orphaned children took shelter there. While they sleep a nurse adds details to the sick bay records.

RIGHT During the Blitz over 177,000 people regularly took shelter in 80 London Underground stations. However, 57 people were killed and 69 injured when a German bomb hit Bank station on 11 January 1940.

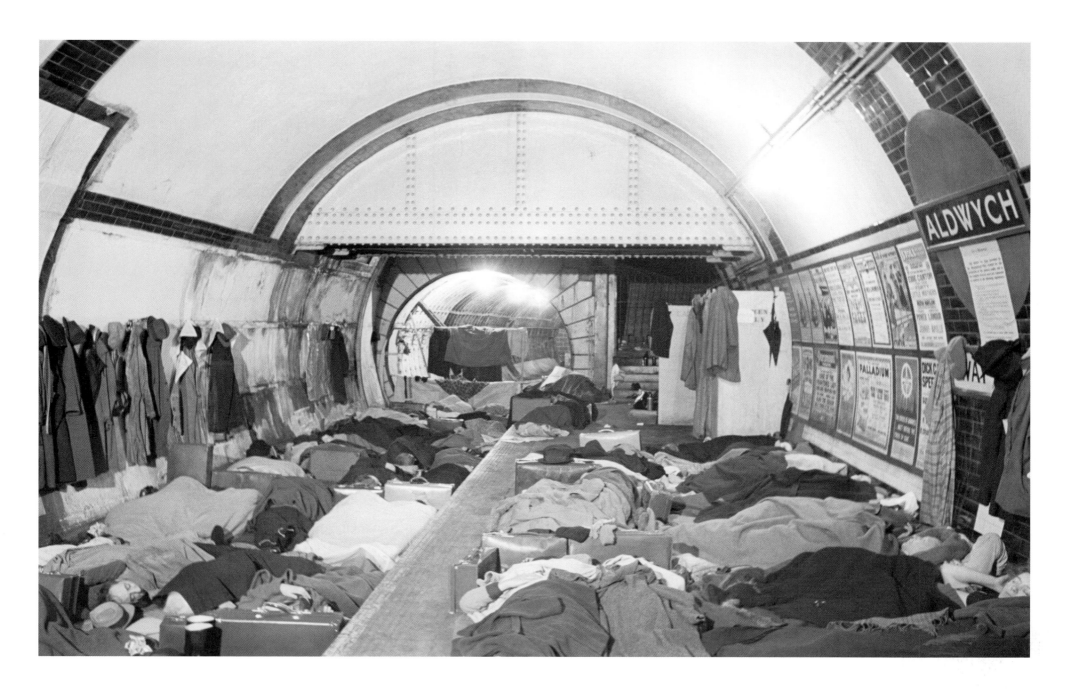

LEFT Builders of the 'Blitz Repair Squad' queue to collect their breakfast from women of the Women's Voluntary Service (WVS) in the mess hut of their camp in London's Onslow Square.

ABOVE Air raid damage in Manchester viewed from the corner of Deansgate and St Mary's Gate, showing burning buildings with firefighting in progress. National Fire Service vehicles are shown in the foreground.

LEFT A group of children arrive on a platform at Brent station, near Kingsbridge, Devon, after being evacuated from Bristol in 1940. The train on which they have travelled can be seen alongside. The children are carrying bags, suitcases or bundles of clothing. They also have their gas masks with them. The guard from the train and many of the female volunteers that helped to escort these children to Devon are also on the platform.

RIGHT Established in June 1939 to serve with the RAF, although not as aircrew, the Women's Auxiliary Air Force (WAAF) was given as one of its primary duties the manning of hydrogen-filled barrage balloons. Heavy steel cables dangled from the balloon and could slice the wing off any aircraft that touched them. This danger forced enemy bombers to fly high above the balloons, making bombing more difficult and at the same time giving anti-aircraft gunners more time to take aim. Large numbers of barrage balloons were used to protect cities, factories, ports and harbours. The training station at Cardington, Bedfordshire, was the RAF's No 1 Balloon Training Unit, and it is here that the aircraftwomen pictured are learning handling techniques; July 1941.

LEFT The Battle of Britain was not just fought by daring young airmen in the skies, but also by bureaucrats on the ground. Civil servants had to organize the conscription of men into the armed forces and women into the factories, the evacuation of children, rationing, the care of the wounded, the housing of those who had been bombed out, the clearing of bomb damage, the supply of airfields, army depots and naval bases, and cope with a thousand unforeseen emergencies.

RIGHT Men of the Auxiliary Fire Service leap from their beds, where they have been dozing in full kit. Grabbing their steel helmets as they go, they respond to another alarm call. During the Blitz over 800 firemen were killed and 7,000 injured.

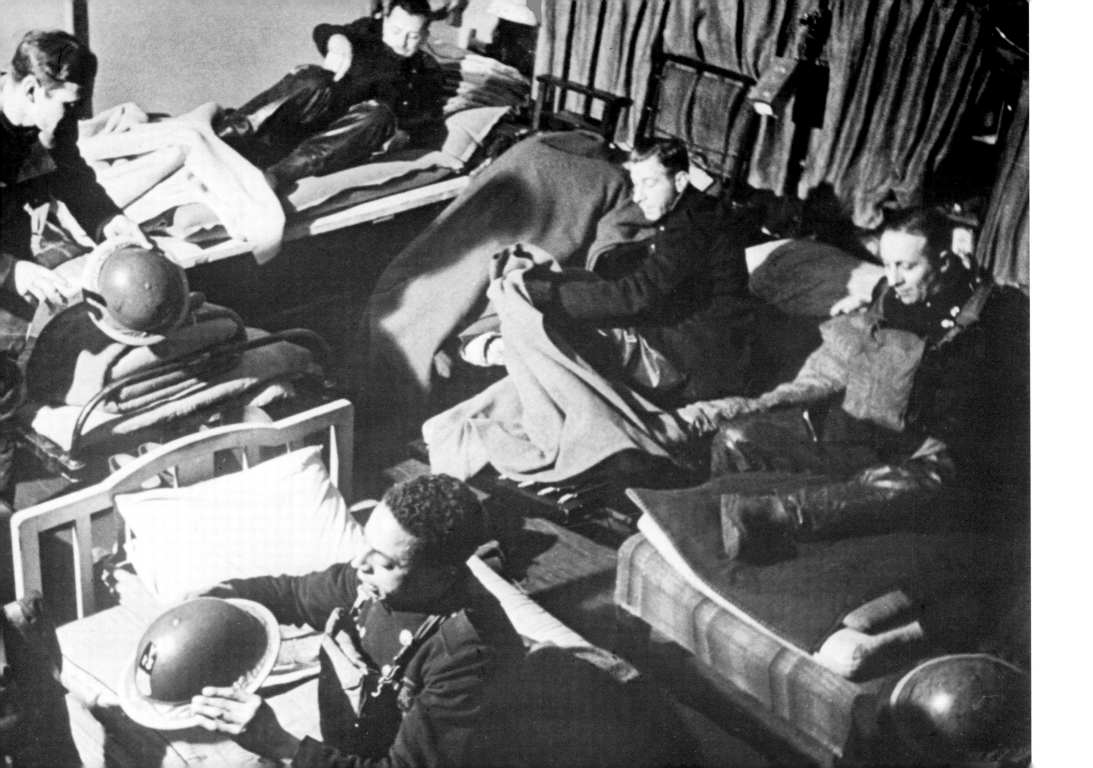

LEFT Members of the London Fire Brigade try to contain a blaze in Queen Victoria Street, EC4, after the last and heaviest major raid mounted on the capital during the Blitz. For six hours on the night of 10–11 May 1941, aircraft of the Luftwaffe dropped over 1,000 tons of bombs on London, claiming 1,486 lives, destroying 11,000 houses and damaging some of the most important historical buildings, including the Houses of Parliament, the British Museum and St James' Palace. The low tide and more than 40 fractured mains deprived the firefighters of water and many of the 2,000 fires blazed out of control.

RIGHT The men of the Auxiliary Fire Service at work in London in 1940. The officer in charge at the scene of a fire tells a despatch rider that there are people trapped in the basement of a bombed building. The despatch rider would then relay the information to headquarters and the medical services. The auxiliaries were unpaid volunteers who trained and fought fires in their spare time, though they were recompensed for lost earnings.

RIGHT Auxiliary Firemen Richard Southern (left) and R.H. Betts work together to fight a fire in the rubble-strewn streets of London in 1940.

FAR LEFT A Bomb Disposal Officer defuses a German bomb that was dropped by a Heinkel on to the fishing trawler *Strath Blare* on 8 March 1941.

LEFT Police and Army bomb disposal officers with a defused German 1,000-kilogram *Luftmine* – or parachute mine – in Glasgow on 18 March 1941.

BELOW The controlled detonation of a German bomb, which fell on the parade ground at RAF Hemswell, Lincolnshire, on 27 August 1940. The bomb did not explode, but buried itself deep in the ground where it was subsequently destroyed by the Station Armament Officer.

ABOVE Men of the Auxiliary Fire Service play their hose on the rubble of a bomb-damaged building in a London street, while engineers from the London Electric Supply Corporation work among the debris to reconnect the electricity supply following an air raid.

RIGHT Tea and buns are supplied by local Air Raid Precautions workers to fellow ARP workers and civilians in this basement shelter in south-east London. The boy with the tray of mugs wears a steel helmet with the letter 'SP' indicating that he is part of a Stretcher Party, while others can be identified as wardens by the 'W' on their helmet. This photograph was taken in November 1940.

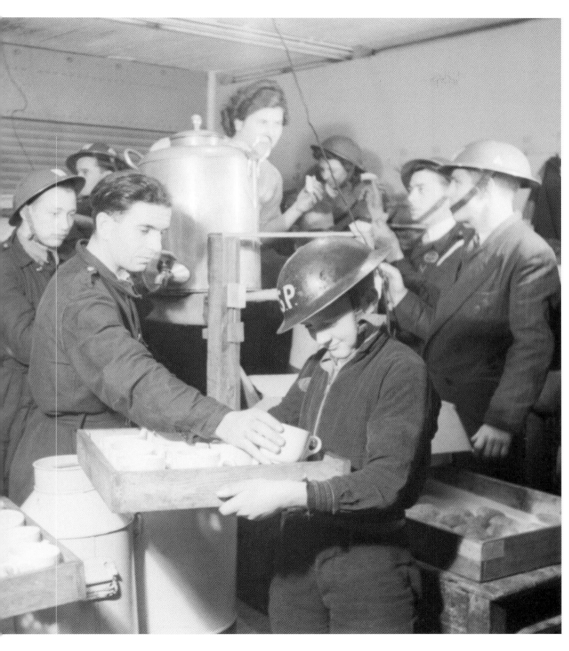

ABOVE Auxiliary Fireman Brian Montagnol Gilks carries a casualty over his shoulders as he leaves a bomb-damaged building during a 'shout' - or call to duty - in London.

LEFT Signboards mark the sites of the shops that once stood on High Street in Exeter before they were bombed out and demolished in the Blitz. Nothing is left but rubble. However, the businesses continue and the signs give their new location.

RIGHT The scene of devastation after an air raid in Birmingham in 1940. All major cities in Britain were hit during the winter of 1940-41, many of them several times. Raids continued, albeit on a decreasing scale, until well into 1944.

BELOW In the Blitz, over 43,000 civilians were killed, 137,000 injured and more than a million houses destroyed or damaged.

ABOVE A Women's Voluntary Service mobile canteen in London in 1941. They supplied tea and something to eat to rescue workers and those bombed out.

LEFT The parents of evacuated children tried to visit as often as possible. Mrs Carter has travelled from London to Haywards Heath in Sussex to enjoy a Sunday lunch with her children Michael and Angela (seated either side of her at the table), who are staying with other evacuees in the home of Mrs Cluton, seen here serving potatoes to Michael.

RIGHT Following a bombing raid, a bus lies in a crater in Balham, south London. Despite the damage, the city continued functioning.

LEFT Readers choosing books which are still amazingly intact among the charred timbers of the Holland House library in London.

RIGHT An artist sits in the rubble of the City of London painting St Paul's Cathedral on 10 October 1941. Although the cathedral had been hit the previous year, it appears undamaged.

THE FINAL VICTORY

Goering was encouraged to switch his bombers to attack cities by air reconnaissance photos showing heavy damage to most of the RAF fighter bases. But while the Luftwaffe estimated the damage would take 4 weeks to repair, most bases were back in operation after two or three days. Almost unnoticed by the Luftwaffe, the RAF recovered. Indeed, so many RAF aircraft remained in the air that the German navy refused to launch the invasion.

The invasion of Britain was postponed, then cancelled as autumn storms swept up the Channel. Hitler could have tried again the following year. But he had other plans. On 22 June 1941, he attacked the Soviet Union. This was a disastrous mistake. Though the German army thrust deep into Russia, it was ill-prepared for the Russian winter. The advance was halted at Stalingrad in the summer of 1942. The following February, the German Sixth Army was surrounded and surrendered. From there the Soviet Army pushed the Germans back all the way to Berlin.

On land the British and Germans fought it out in North Africa, while the RAF began a bombing campaign against Germany. After a key victory at El Alamein in October 1942, the Germans were eventually forced out of North Africa. By then, the Japanese had attacked Pearl Harbor, bringing America into the war.

Allied forces then landed on Sicily and in Italy. On 6 June 1944, the Allies landed in Normandy. They fought their way across Western Europe. When the Soviets took Berlin, Hitler committed suicide and Germany surrendered.

If the Battle of Britain had been lost and Britain had been invaded, the consequences would have been dire. There would have been no base for the Allies to launch the D-Day landings, and the US and Canada would have been left surrounded by a Nazi-controlled Atlantic, a Japanese-controlled Pacific and countries led by Nazi sympathizers to the south in Latin America. With the full military might of Germany committed in the east, the Soviet Union would have capitulated and Germany would have won the war. As it was, Britain was on the winning side.

A vast crowd gathers outside Buckingham Palace and cheers as the Royal family come out on to the balcony during the VE Day celebrations on 8 May 1945.

LEFT General Ernst Udet, shown at the controls of his aircraft, took the blame for the Luftwaffe's failure to win a decisive victory in the Battle of Britain.

BELOW Udet's suicide on 17 November 1941 was hushed up and he was given a hero's funeral in the presence of Hitler and Goering. The Knight's Cross party accompanying the gun carriage was led by Lieutenant Colonel Galland.

RIGHT The White Ensign of a Naval Beach Party flies on a Normandy beach on 6 June 1944 – D-Day. From there, British troops moved slowly inland.

LEFT Artillery shelling at Bingen, Mosel. From 11 to 13 March the American Third Army cleaned out the Germans who remained north of the Mosel. They then regrouped and started their attack towards Bingen and Bad Kreuznach to prevent the enemy from retreating across the Rhine. The attack was then to continue southeast to secure a crossing somewhere between Mainz and Worms.

RIGHT Aerial view of the prisoner of war compound at Hamburg, packed with surrendered German troops.

BELOW Surrendered Germans were stripped of their weapons. The Allies kept the arms nearby in case war broke out against the Soviets.

LEFT The Reichstag after the Allied bombing of Berlin. British and American bombers reduced German cities to rubble.

LEFT Admiral Dönitz in the custody of the British Army after his arrest. Hitler's chosen successor after his death on 30 April 1945, Dönitz negotiated the capitulation of German Forces in the west.

RIGHT The German occupation force in Norway gave up without a fight. As prisoners, they were processed at a camp in Elverum ready to be shipped back to Germany in 1945. Then they were moved to an embarkation camp at Mandal where they are pictured playing cards.

BELOW Four years of occupation were over for much of western Europe. Though privations would continue, peace and prosperity were at hand.

FAR LEFT Although the Free French were only a small component of the invasion force, they were allowed to lead the liberation of Paris.

LEFT British Victory Parade in Berlin: British troops march down the Charlottenburger Chaussee, Berlin.

LEFT At 3pm, the crowd fell silent as Churchill's broadcast was played over loudspeakers in Trafalgar Square.

RIGHT Churchill waves to crowds in Whitehall on 8 May 1945 - VE Day - after he broadcast to the nation, announcing the war against Germany had been won, although the war against Japan continued. In the speech he gave from the balcony, he said:

"This is your victory! It is the victory of the cause of freedom in every land. In all our long history we have never seen a greater day than this. Everyone, man or woman, has done their best. Everyone has tried. Neither the long years, nor the dangers, nor the fierce attacks of the enemy, have in any way weakened the independent resolve of the British nation. God bless you all."

INDEX

A

Adams, Sir Ronald F. 28
air bases
    attacks on 113, 121, 122
air raid precautions 146-9, 186-7
Air Sea Rescue Service 120
Air Transport Auxiliary (ATA) service
    31, 107
Allen, J. L. 132
Amsterdam 8-9
Anderson shelters 160-1
Arbuthnot, J. 133
Auxiliary Fire Service 180-3, 186

B

Bader, Douglas 131, 134-5
Balham 191
Ball, G. E. 134
Beadnell Bay 28
Beaumont, Belgium 8
Beaverbrook, Lord 40
Belgium 6, 8
Bentley Priory 102, 104, 105, 111
Bergman, V. 74
Berlin 200, 202-3
Betts, R. H. 183
Biggin Hill 53, 119
Birdcage Walk, London 44
Birmingham 40, 189
Blake, A. G. 57
Blitz 97, 155, 158-61, 162-7, 173-7, 180-3,
    186-7, 189, 191-3
bomb disposal 184-5
Borman, Martin 18
Boulton, J. E. 74
Brauchitsch, Walter von 20-1

Breker, Arno 18
Brinsden, F. N. 57
Bristol Blenheims
    Mark IV 60
Britain
    declares war on Germany 6
    planned invasion of 15, 20-1, 24-5, 194
    preparations for invasion 22-3, 26-31,
    32-7
British Expeditionary Force (BEF) 6,
    10-11, 12-15, 16-17, 18-19
Brown, Ben 134
Bruckner, Wilhelm 18
Buckingham Palace 166-7, 195

C

Cabinet War Rooms 110
Café de Paris, Piccadilly 158
Camm, Sydney 50
Campbell, Neil 134
Castle Bromwich 40, 50
Chain Home system 115, 116-17
Chamberlain, Neville 6
Churchill, Winston 6, 11, 15, 22, 30, 34, 40,
    110, 122, 144, 204, 205
Clowes, A. V. Taffy 69
Clyde, W. P. 64
Coast Watch (Royal Navy) 23, 29
Coltishall, Norfolk 139
Cozens, H. I. 50
Crossley, Winifred 31
Crowley-Milling, Dennis 134
Croydon 119
Cruiser Mk IV tank 10-11
Cunningham, W. 57
Cunnison, Margaret 31

Czechoslovakia 6

D

D-Day landings 196-7
Darley, H. S. 140
Deere, A. C. 133
Defiants 50, 62, 63, 67, 119
Denmark 6
Dietrich, Otto 18
'Dig for Victory' campaign 153
Digby, Lincolnshire 52
Dönitz, Karl 171, 200
Dorniers
    17Zs 88-9
    Do 17 78, 82, 89, 100, 116
Dover 16-17, 18-19, 32-3
Dowding, Sir Hugh 102, 104, 106, 111, 122
Dunkirk 12-15, 25
Duperier, Lieutenant 137
Duxford, Cambridgeshire 118

E

Eastleigh 40
Elizabeth, Queen 104, 166-7
Eltham 45
evacuees 178, 190
Exeter 188-9

F

Faireys 59, 60-1
Fairweather, Margaret 31
Fechtner, E. 74
Feric, Miroslaw 75
Finucane, Brendan 'Paddy' 55
'Finger Four' formation 50-1, 86
formations 50-3, 86

Fowlmere, Cambridgeshire 54, 56-7,
    71, 73
France 6, 8, 10-11, 202
Franco-Belgian Air Training School,
    Odiham 59
Friedlander, Mona 31
Furst, B. 74, 76

G

Galland, Adolf 84-5, 196
George VI, King 104, 132, 166-7
Giesler, Herman 18
Gieves & Hawkes 165
Gilks, Brian Montagnol 187
Goering, Hermann 25, 78, 81, 83, 87, 194
Gordon, Mary 154
Gosport 161
Goth, W. 74
Gower, Pauline 31
Grier, T. 64
Grimsby 34
Grzeszczak, Jan 75
Guildhall, London 164

H

Hallows, H. J. L. 133
Hamburg 199
Harvard Mark I 46-7
Heinkel
    He 111 78, 93, 96, 97, 140, 141, 144
    He 59 101
Henneberg, Zdzislaw 75
Hitler, Adolf 6, 11, 15, 18, 20-1, 78, 144, 194
Home Guard 15, 22, 36, 42-3, 49, 150
Hubert, Brigadier 28
Hughes, Joan 31

Hurricanes
    Mark I 58, 65, 128-9
    Mark Is 58, 124-5, 127
    production of 41, 50, 58
    role of 76

J

Janduch, S. 74
Jeffries, J. 74
Jennings, B. J. 71
JG 2 98
JG 26 84-5
JG 3 84
JG 53 80-1
Johnson, J. E. 131
Junkers
    Ju-87 96
    Ju88 78, 90-1
    Ju88A-1 92

K

Kaucky, J. 74
Keitel, Wilhelm 18, 20-1
Kensington Gardens 153
Kent, J. A. 75
Kesselring, Albert 81
Kirton-in-Lindsey, Lincolnshire 62, 63,
    67

L

Lane, B. I. E. 'Sandy' 56
Le Neubourg, France 10-11
Leathart, J. A. 132
Leigh-Mallory, Trafford 107
Lewis, Albert 'Zulu' 125
Lille-Seclin, France 102-3

Liverpool 170-1
Lockheed Hudson 13
Lodz, Poland 7
London
 Blitz 97, 116, 144, 155, 158-61, 162-7, 173-7, 180-3, 186-7, 189, 191-3
 defences for 44-5, 148-50
Luftwaffe 78
Lützow, Gunther 84

M
Malan, Adolph 'Sailor' 52, 128, 129, 132
Maly, J. 74
Manchester 156-7, 177
Manor Farm, Fowlmere 56-7
Maplethorpe 37
McKnight, Lidstone 'Willie' 126, 134
McNab, E. A. 127
Meissner, Otto 18
Messerschmitt
 Bf 109 78, 80-1, 94-5, 98
 Bf 110 78-9, 99, 142, 143
Miller, R. F. G. 140
Mitchell, Reginald 50
Mölders, Werner 86, 87
Morrison shelters 172-3
Mosel 198
Mouchotte, Rene 137

N
Netherlands 6, 8-9
North Weald, Essex 58
Northumbria 28
Norway 201

O

Odiham, Hampshire 59
Operation Sealion 15, 24-5, 194
Osterley Park 22, 43

P

Paris 11, 18, 202
Park, Keith 106
Patterson, Gabrielle 31
Pétain, Philippe 11, 22
Petticoat Lane market 168
pilots
 Australian 136
 Czechoslovak 70-1, 74, 76, 77
 equipment for 109
 Free French 59, 137
 German 78
 image of 50
 Polish 75
 scrambling 139
 training 46-8
Plenderleith, R. 133
Plymouth 35
Poland 6, 7
'Pooh' (gun emplacement) 32
Poulson, Martin 158
Primrose Hill 149
Puda, R. 74
Pym, Captain 110

R

radar 102, 112, 114-15, 116
rationing 169
Raeder, Erich 20-1
Rees, Rosemary 31
Reynaud, Paul 11
Rip (dog) 146

Roberts, Fred 71
Rossiwal, Theodor 99
Royal Air Force
 fighters available 50
 pilot shortage 122
 tactics 50-3
Royal Artillery 27
Royal Hospital, Chelsea 148
Royal Navy
 Coast Watch 23, 29
Rypl, F. 74

S

Saarland 6
St. Margaret's, Dover 32-3
St. Paul's Cathedral 162-3, 193
Sangatte 81
'Saucepans for Spitfires' campaign 39-9
Sandgate 26
Savill, J. E. 134
Schalk, John 99
Seda, K. 74
Sheerness 27
Simpson, J. W. 133
Sinclair, G. L. 74
sound locators 112
Southern, Richard 183
Southwark 159
Soviet Union 6
Speer, Albert 18
Speidel, Wilhelm 81
Spitfires 122-3
 at Castle Bromwich factory 50
 at Eastleigh factory 40, 50
 Mark I 68, 140
 Mark Is 51, 54

Mark IAs 53
 production of 50, 58
 role of 76
 turnaround time 73
Squadrons:
 III Squadron 124-5
 19 Squadron 54, 56-7, 73
 43 Squadron 133
 56 Squadron 58
 85 Squadron 142
 87 Squadron 102-3
 242 (Canadian) Squadron 126, 134-5
 257 Squadron 128-9, 130, 139
 264 Squadron 62, 63, 67
 303 (Polish) Squadron 75
 310 (Czechoslovak) Squadron 70-1, 74, 76, 77
 401 Squadron 127
 452 Squadron 136
 601 Squadron 64-5, 72
 610 Squadron 53, 66
 611 Squadron 52, 68
 615 Squadron 108
Stanford Tuck, Robert 28, 130, 132, 139
Staples, M. E. 143
Stumpff, Hans-Jürgen 86
Suter, Alan 160
Suter, Doris 160

T

Tamblyn, Hugh 134
Tedder, Lord 106
Townsend, P. W. 133
Trafalgar Square 204
Turner, Stan 134

U
Udet, Ernst 86, 196
Upton, H. C. 133

V
VE day celebrations 195, 203, 204-5
'Victory' formation 53, 86
Vopalecuy, J. 74

W
Wellingtons 61
West Ham 116
Weygand, Maxime 11
Wilberforce, Marion 31
'Winnie' (gun emplacement) 32, 33
Wintringham, Tom 22
Wolff, Karl 18
Women's Auxiliary Air Force (WAAF) 179
Women's Land Army 152
Worthing 26
Wyton, Cambridgeshire 113

Z
Zima, R. 74
Zimprich, S. 74
Zumbach, Jan 75

PICTURE CREDITS